Keep your love
and po

W9-AFY-932

THE ARDEN SHAKESPEARE
BOOK OF QUOTATIONS
ON

Love

Compiled by
JANE ARMSTRONG

AS

The Arden website is at
http://www.ardenshakespeare.com

First published 2001 by The Arden Shakespeare

This Collection Copyright © 2001 Jane Armstrong

Arden Shakespeare is an imprint of Thomson Learning

Thomson Learning
Berkshire House
168–173 High Holborn
London WC1V 7AA

Designed and typeset by Martin Bristow

Printed in Singapore by Seng Lee Press

British Library Cataloguing in Publication Data
A catalogue record for this book is available from the
British Library

Library of Congress Cataloguing in Publication Data
A catalogue record has been requested

ISBN 1-903436-50-8

NPN 9 8 7 6 5 4 3 2 1

Love

THE ARDEN SHAKESPEARE
BOOKS OF QUOTATIONS

Life

Love

Death

Nature

Songs & Sonnets

The Seven Ages of Man

Falling in Love

Spirit of love, how quick and fresh art thou.

Twelfth Night 1.1.9

The very instant that I saw you did
My heart fly to your service.

Tempest 3.1.64–5

At the first sight
They have changed eyes.

Tempest 1.2.441–2

In silent wonder of still-gazing eyes.

Lucrece 84

[5]

I was won . . . With the first glance.

Troilus and Cressida 3.2.114–15

Who ever loved that loved not at first sight?

As You Like It 3.5.82

For your brother and my sister no sooner met,
but they looked; no sooner looked, but they loved;
no sooner loved, but they sighed; no sooner sighed,
but they asked one another the reason; no sooner knew
the reason, but they sought the remedy.

As You Like It 5.2.32–7

Are you a god? would you create me new?

Comedy of Errors 3.2.39

[6]

'LOVE, WHOSE MONTH IS EVER MAY'

Love's Labour's Lost 4.3.99

It was a lover and his lass,
    With a hey and a ho and a hey nonino,
That o'er the green corn-field did pass,
    In spring-time, the only pretty ring-time,
When birds do sing, hey ding a ding, ding,
Sweet lovers love the spring.

As You Like It 5.3.15–20

O, how this spring of love resembleth
The uncertain glory of an April day,
Which now shows all the beauty of the sun,
And by and by a cloud takes all away.

Two Gentlemen of Verona 1.3.84–7

This bud of love, by summer's ripening breath,
May prove a beauteous flower when next we meet.

Romeo and Juliet 2.2.121–2

O, she doth teach the torches to burn bright.
It seems she hangs upon the cheek of night
As a rich jewel in an Ethiop's ear –
Beauty too rich for use, for earth too dear.

Romeo and Juliet 1.5.44–7

Let every eye negotiate for itself,
And trust no agent; for beauty is a witch
Against whose charms faith melteth into blood.

Much Ado About Nothing 2.1.169–71

Being in Love

What did he when thou saw'st him? What said he?
How looked he? Wherein went he? What makes he
here? Did he ask for me? Where remains he?
How parted he with thee? And when shalt thou
see him again? Answer me in one word.

As You Like It 3.2.217–21

JAQUES What stature is she of?
ORLANDO Just as high as my heart.

As You Like It 3.2.265–6

O coz, coz, coz, my pretty little coz, that thou didst
know how many fathom deep I am in love!

As You Like It 4.1.197–8

[9]

Prove true, imagination, O prove true.

Twelfth Night 3.4.374

The prize of all-too-precious you.

Sonnet 86

Thinking of nothing else, putting all affairs else
in oblivion, as if there were nothing else to be done
but to see him.

2 Henry IV 5.5.25–7

I am to wait, though waiting so be hell,
Not blame your pleasure be it ill or well.

Sonnet 58

Silence is the perfectest herald of joy; I were but
little happy, if I could say how much.

Much Ado About Nothing 2.1.288–9

If it were now to die
'Twere now to be most happy, for I fear
My soul hath her content so absolute
That not another comfort like to this
Succeeds in unknown fate.

Othello 2.1.187–91

Come what sorrow can,
It cannot countervail the exchange of joy
That one short minute gives me in her sight.

Romeo and Juliet 2.6.3–5

Time goes on crutches till love hath all his rites.

Much Ado About Nothing 2.1.336–7

She loved me for the dangers I had passed
And I loved her that she did pity them.

Othello 1.3.168–9

Speak low, if you speak love.

Much Ado About Nothing 2.1.91

O Beauty,
Till now I never knew thee.

Henry VIII 1.4.75–6

If thou remember'st not the slightest folly
That ever love did make thee run into,
Thou hast not loved.

As You Like It 2.4.32–4

ROSALIND Not true in love?
CELIA Yes, when he is in, but I think he is not in.

As You Like It 3.4.25–6

Mistress, know yourself. Down on your knees
And thank heaven, fasting, for a good man's love;
For I must tell you friendly in your ear,
Sell when you can, you are not for all markets.

As You Like It 3.5.57–60

What is Love? . . .

Love is a smoke made with the fume of sighs;
Being purged, a fire sparkling in lovers' eyes;
Being vexed, a sea nourished with lovers' tears;
What is it else? A madness most discreet,
A choking gall, and a preserving sweet.

Romeo and Juliet 1.1.190–4

Love is a spirit all compact of fire.

Venus and Adonis 149

Is love a tender thing? It is too rough,
Too rude, too boisterous, and it pricks like thorn.

Romeo and Juliet 1.4.25–6

What love can do, that dares love attempt.

Romeo and Juliet 2.2.68

Love is too young to know what conscience is.

Sonnet 151

Love will not be spurred to what it loathes.

Two Gentlemen of Verona 5.2.7

There's beggary in the love that can be reckoned.

Antony and Cleopatra 1.1.15

Tell me where is Fancy bred,
Or in the heart, or in the head?
How begot, how nourished? . . .
It is engendered in the eyes.

Merchant of Venice 3.2.63–5, 67

Love, first learned in a lady's eyes,
Lives not alone immured in the brain
But with the motion of all elements
Courses as swift as thought in every power
And gives to every power a double power,
Above their functions and their offices.

Love's Labour's Lost 4.3.301–6

Love looks not with the eyes, but with the mind,
And therefore is winged Cupid painted blind.

Midsummer Night's Dream 1.1.234–5

. . . 'Tis not hereafter

I did love you once.

Hamlet 3.1.115

My Oberon! What visions have I seen!
Methought I was enamoured of an ass.

Midsummer Night's Dream 4.1.75–6

Time qualifies the spark and fire of it.

Hamlet 4.7.113

That time . . .
When love, converted from the thing it was,
Shall reasons find of settled gravity.

Sonnet 49

[17]

The Course of True Love . . .

The course of true love never did run smooth

Midsummer Night's Dream 1.1.134

A pair of star-crossed lovers.

Romeo and Juliet Prologue 6

She never told her love,
But let concealment like a worm i'th' bud
Feed on her damask cheek: she pined in thought,
And with a green and yellow melancholy
She sat like Patience on a monument,
Smiling at grief. Was not this love indeed?

Twelfth Night 2.4.111–16

Prosperity's the very bond of love,
Whose fresh complexion and whose heart together
Affliction alters.

Winter's Tale 4.4.575–7

That thou hast her it is not all my grief,
And yet it may be said I loved her dearly;
That she hath thee is of my wailing chief,
A loss in love that touches me more nearly.
Loving offenders, thus I will excuse ye:
Thou dost love her, because thou knowst I love her,
And for my sake even so doth she abuse me,
Suff'ring my friend for my sake to approve her;
If I lose thee, my loss is my love's gain,
And losing her, my friend hath found that loss;
Both find each other, and I lose both twain,
And both for my sake lay on me this cross:
    But here's the joy, my friend and I are one;
    Sweet flattery! Then she loves but me alone.

Sonnet 42

My love is as a fever, longing still
For that which longer nurseth the disease,
Feeding on that which doth preserve the ill,
Th'uncertain sickly appetite to please:
My reason, the physician to my love,
Angry that his prescriptions are not kept,
Hath left me, and I, desperate, now approve
Desire is death, which physic did except.
Past cure I am, now reason is past care,
And frantic mad with ever more unrest;
My thoughts and my discourse as madmen's are,
At random from the truth vainly expressed:
   For I have sworn thee fair, and thought thee bright,
   Who art as black as hell, as dark as night.

Sonnet 147

   Beware . . . of jealousy!
It is the green-eyed monster, which doth mock
The meat it feeds on.

Othello 3.3.167–9

I saw her first.

Two Noble Kinsmen 2.2.160

Trifles light as air
Are to the jealous confirmations strong
As proofs of holy writ.

Othello 3.3.325–7

This is the very ecstasy of love,
Whose violent property fordoes itself
And leads the will to desperate undertakings.

Hamlet 2.1.103–5

One that loved not wisely, but too well.

Othello 5.2.344

[21]

ABSENCE

This great gap of time
My Antony is away.

Antony and Cleopatra 1.5.5–6

How like a winter hath my absence been
From thee, the pleasure of the fleeting year!
What freezings have I felt, what dark days seen,
What old December's bareness everywhere!
And yet this time removed was summer's time,
The teeming autumn big with rich increase
Bearing the wanton burthen of the prime,
Like widowed wombs after their lords' decease:
Yet this abundant issue seemed to me
But hope of orphans, and unfathered fruit;
For summer and his pleasures wait on thee,
And thou away, the very birds are mute;
 Or, if they sing, 'tis with so dull a cheer
 That leaves look pale, dreading the winter's near.

Sonnet 97

O never say that I was false of heart,
Though absence seemed my flame to qualify;
As easy might I from myself depart
As from my soul which in thy breast doth lie:
That is my home of love; if I have ranged,
Like him that travels I return again;
Just to the time, not with the time exchanged,
So that myself bring water for my stain;
Never believe, though in my nature reigned
All frailties that besiege all kinds of blood,
That it could so preposterously be stained,
To leave for nothing all thy sum of good:
    For nothing this wide universe I call,
    Save thou, my rose; in it thou art my all.

Sonnet 109

Comforted . . .
That there is this jewel in the world
That I may see again.

Cymbeline 1.2.21–3

[23]

Unreciprocated Love

'Twere all one
That I should love a bright particular star
And think to wed it, he is so above me.

All's Well That Ends Well 1.1.86–8

Who taught thee how to make me love thee more,
The more I hear and see just cause of hate?

Sonnet 150

The nobleman would have dealt with her like a
nobleman, and she sent him away as cold as a snowball.

Pericles 4.6.136–8

INFIDELITY

Nay, pray you seek no colour for your going,
But bid farewell and go.

Antony and Cleopatra 1.3.33–4

It is a greater grief
To bear love's wrong, than hate's known injury.

Sonnet 40

In Venice they do let God see the pranks
They dare not show their husbands; their best conscience
Is not to leave't undone, but keep't unknown.

Othello 3.3.205–7

Sigh no more, ladies, sigh no more,
Men were deceivers ever.

Much Ado About Nothing 2.3.61–2

When my love swears that she is made of truth,
I do believe her, though I know she lies.

Sonnet 138

She's gone, I am abused, and my relief
Must be to loathe her.

Othello 3.3.271–2

If beauty have a soul, this is not she.

Troilus and Cressida 5.2.145

Lovers

Love is blind, and lovers cannot see
The pretty follies that themselves commit.

Merchant of Venice 2.6.36–7

At lovers' perjuries,
They say, Jove laughs.

Romeo and Juliet 2.2.92–3

Lovers break not hours,
Unless it be to come before their time.

Two Gentlemen of Verona 5.1.4–5

MEN AND WOMEN IN LOVE

Men have died from time to time and worms have
eaten them, but not for love.

As You Like It 4.1.101–2

Tricks he hath had in him, which gentlemen have . . .
He did love her, sir as a gentleman loves a woman . . .
He loved her, sir, and loved her not.

All's Well That Ends Well 5.3.239–48

Cleopatra hath
Nodded him to her.

Antony and Cleopatra 3.6.66–7

The triple pillar of the world transformed
Into a strumpet's fool.

Antony and Cleopatra 1.1.12–13

Think you there was or might be such a man
As this I dreamt of?

Antony and Cleopatra 5.2.92–3

A kind heart he hath: a woman would run through fire
and water for such a kind heart.

Merry Wives of Windsor 3.4.100–1

It is a holiday to look on them. Lord,
the difference of men!

Two Noble Kinsmen 2.1.55–6

JULIA They do not love that do not show their love.
LUCETTA O, they love least that let men know their
love.

Two Gentlemen of Verona 1.2.31–2

We cannot fight for love, as men may do;
We should be wooed, and were not made to woo.

Midsummer Night's Dream 2.1.241–2

Dumb jewels often in their silent kind,
More than quick words, do move a woman's mind.

Two Gentlemen of Verona 3.1.90–1

Sex

———

There's not a minute of our lives should stretch
    Without some pleasure now.

    Antony and Cleopatra 1.1.47–8

Eternity was in our lips and eyes,
Bliss in our brows' bent; none our parts so poor
But was a race of heaven.

    Antony and Cleopatra 1.3.36–8

    The nobleness of life
Is to do thus, when such a mutual pair
And such a twain can do't.

    Antony and Cleopatra 1.1.37–9

We have kissed away
Kingdoms and provinces.

Antony and Cleopatra 3.10.7–8

The barge she sat in, like a burnished throne
Burned on the water; the poop was beaten gold;
Purple the sails, and so perfumed that
The winds were love-sick with them; the oars were silver,
Which to the tune of flutes kept stroke, and made
The water which they beat to follow faster,
As amorous of their strokes. For her own person,
It beggared all description: she did lie
In her pavilion, cloth-of-gold of tissue,
O'erpicturing that Venus where we see
The fancy outwork nature. On each side her
Stood pretty dimpled boys, like smiling cupids,
With divers-coloured fans, whose wind did seem
To glow the delicate cheeks which they did cool,
And what they undid did.

Antony and Cleopatra 2.2.201–15

Desire my pilot is, beauty my prize.

Lucrece 279

Age cannot wither her, nor custom stale
Her infinite variety. Other women cloy
The appetites they feed, but she makes hungry
Where most she satisfies.

Antony and Cleopatra 2.2.245–8

She looks like sleep,
As she would catch another Antony
In her strong toil of grace.

Antony and Cleopatra 5.2.344–6

On her left breast
A mole cinque-spotted: like the crimson drops
I'th' bottom of a cowslip.

Cymbeline 2.2.37–9

Love keeps his revels where there are but twain.

Venus and Adonis 123

Lovers can see to do their amorous rites
By their own beauties.

Romeo and Juliet 3.2.8–9

Incorporate then they seem, face grows to face.

Venus and Adonis 540

She would hang on him
As if increase of appetite had grown
By what it fed on.

Hamlet 1.2.143–5

Now is she in the very lists of love,
Her champion mounted for the hot encounter.

Venus and Adonis 595–6

Do not give dalliance
Too much the rein. The strongest oaths are straw
To th' fire in th' blood.

Tempest 4.1.51–3

They are in the very wrath of love, and they will
together. Clubs cannot part them.

As You Like It 5.2.39–41

The beast with two backs.

Othello 1.1.115

Women are angels, wooing;
Things won are done.

Troilus and Cressida 1.2.279–80

What win I if I gain the thing I seek?
A dream, a breath, a froth of fleeting joy.
Who . . . sells eternity to get a toy?

Lucrece 211–12, 14

[36]

Th'expense of spirit in a waste of shame
Is lust in action; and till action, lust
Is perjured, murd'rous, bloody, full of blame,
Savage, extreme, rude, cruel, not to trust;
Enjoyed no sooner but despised straight;
Past reason hunted, and no sooner had,
Past reason hated as a swallowed bait,
On purpose laid to make the taker mad;
Mad in pursuit, and in possession so,
Had, having, and in quest to have, extreme;
A bliss in proof, and proved, a very woe;
Before, a joy proposed; behind, a dream.
    All this the world well knows, yet none knows well
    To shun the heaven that leads men to this hell.

Sonnet 129

COUNTESS Tell me the reason why thou wilt marry.
CLOWN My poor body, madam, requires it; I am driven
   on by the flesh, and he must needs go that the devil
   drives.

All's Well That Ends Well 1.3.27–30

This momentary joy breeds months of pain;
This hot desire converts to cold disdain.

Lucrece 690–1

This is the monstruosity in love . . . , that the will is
infinite and the execution confined; that the desire
is boundless and the act a slave to limit.

Troilus and Cressida 3.2.79–81

Love comforteth like sunshine after rain,
But lust's effect is tempest after sun;
Love's gentle spring doth always fresh remain,
Lust's winter comes ere summer half be done;
Love surfeits not, lust like a glutton dies;
Love is all truth, lust full of forged lies.

Venus and Adonis 799–804

Expressions of Love

You alone are you.

Sonnet 84

Shall I compare thee to a summer's day?
Thou art more lovely and more temperate:
Rough winds do shake the darling buds of May,
And summer's lease hath all too short a date:
Sometime too hot the eye of heaven shines,
And often is his gold complexion dimmed;
And every fair from fair sometime declines,
By chance or nature's changing course untrimmed:
But thy eternal summer shall not fade,
Nor lose possession of that fair thou ow'st,
Nor shall death brag thou wander'st in his shade
When in eternal lines to time thou grow'st:
    So long as men can breathe or eyes can see
    So long lives this, and this gives life to thee.

Sonnet 18

What's in a name? That which we call a rose
By any other word would smell as sweet;
So Romeo would, were he not Romeo called,
Retain that dear perfection which he owes
Without that title.

Romeo and Juliet 2.2.43–7

My bounty is as boundless as the sea,
My love as deep: the more I give to thee
The more I have, for both are infinite.

Romeo and Juliet 2.2.133–5

My five wits, nor my five senses, can
Dissuade one foolish heart from serving thee.

Sonnet 141

I know no ways to mince it in love but directly to say
'I love you.'

Henry V 5.2.126–7

You have witchcraft in your lips.

Henry V 5.2.273

For where thou art, there is the world itself, . . .
And where thou art not, desolation.

2 Henry VI 3.2.362, 364

Since my dear soul was mistress of her choice,
And could of men distinguish her election,
Sh'ath sealed thee for herself.

Hamlet 3.2.64–6

I do love you . . .
Dearer than eyesight, space and liberty.

King Lear 1.1.55–6

Excellent wretch! perdition catch my soul
But I do love thee! and when I love thee not
Chaos is come again.

Othello 3.3.90–2

ARIEL Do you love me, master? No?
PROSPERO Dearly, my delicate Ariel.

Tempest 4.1.48–9

I would not wish
Any companion in the world but you.

Tempest 3.1.54–5

I will live in thy heart, die in thy lap, and be buried in
thy eyes; and moreover, I will go with thee to thy uncle's.

Much Ado About Nothing 5.2.95–7

How silver-sweet sound lovers' tongues by night,
Like softest music to attending ears.

Romeo and Juliet 2.2.165–6

If music be the food of love, play on,
Give me excess of it, that, surfeiting,
The appetite may sicken, and so die.
That strain again, it had a dying fall:
O, it came o'er my ear like the sweet sound
That breathes upon a bank of violets,
Stealing and giving odour.

Twelfth Night 1.1.1–7

What light is light, if Silvia be not seen?
What joy is joy, if Silvia be not by? . . .
Except I be by Silvia in the night,
There is no music in the nightingale.

Two Gentlemen of Verona 3.1.174–5, 178–9

Marriage

Kiss me, Kate, we will be married o' Sunday.

Taming of the Shrew 2.1.318

Jack shall have Jill
Nought shall go ill;
The man shall have his mare again, and all shall be well.

Midsummer Night's Dream 3.2.461–3

Get thee a good husband, and use him as he uses thee.

All's Well That Ends Well 1.1.214–15

If men could be contented to be what they are,
there were no fear in marriage.

All's Well That Ends Well 1.3.50–1

[45]

Hath homely age th'alluring beauty took
From my poor cheek? then he hath wasted it.

Comedy of Errors 2.1.90–1

Thou say'st his meat was sauced with thy upbraidings;
Unquiet meals make ill digestions; . . .
Thou say'st his sports were hindered by thy brawls;
Sweet recreation barred, what doth ensue
But moody and dull melancholy.

Comedy of Errors 5.1.73–4, 77–9

Wars is no strife
To the dark house and the detested wife.

All's Well That Ends Well 2.3.290–1

A young man married is a man that's marred.

All's Well That Ends Well 2.3.297

Hasty marriage seldom proveth well.

3 Henry VI 4.1.18

Thou wilt needs thrust thy neck into a yoke . . .
and sigh away Sundays.

Much Ado About Nothing 1.1.191–2

Thou art sad; get thee a wife, get thee a wife!

Much Ado About Nothing 5.4.121

Love's Eternity

So they loved, as love in twain
Had the essence but in one:
Two distincts, division none.

Phoenix and Turtle 25–7

Let me not to the marriage of true minds
Admit impediments; love is not love
Which alters when it alteration finds,
Or bends with the remover to remove.
O no, it is an ever-fixed mark,
That looks on tempests and is never shaken;
It is the star to every wand'ring bark,
Whose worth's unknown, although his height be taken.
Love's not Time's fool, though rosy lips and cheeks
Within his bending sickle's compass come;
Love alters not with his brief hours and weeks,
But bears it out even to the edge of doom.
   If this be error and upon me proved,
   I never writ, nor no man ever loved.

Sonnet 116